D1015546

Our family has known and loved Tuda Libby Crews for many years, and our hats are off to our ranch and chuckwagon cook and baker friend and her fancy cowboy cookies cookbook.
  —Sue Cunningham and Jean Shepherd Cates, authors of *Chuckwagon Recipes & Others*

Tuda's ranch heritage and true love for the American West and cowboys make this book a real treat. Not only are the cookies beautiful–they are delicious and achievable by all! A great gift book!
  —Karen and Curt Gowdy, Jr.

For Jenni →

Mave fun! Yahoo!

Dueda Libby Crea

Y

00 99 98 97 6 5 4 3 2

Text copyright © 1997 by
Tuda Libby Crews

Photography copyright © 1997 by
Gibbs Smith, Publisher

Published by
Gibbs Smith, Publisher
P.O.Box 667
Layton, Utah 84041

Book design and composition by
Scott Van Kampen
Photography by
Jan Schou of
Borge Andersen Associates
Other photographs as credited
Book edited by
Caroll McKanna Shreeve

Printed and bound in Korea

**Library of Congress
Cataloging-in-Publication Data**

Crews, Tuda Libby
Wild, wild west cowboy cookies / by
Tuda Libby Crews, – 1st ed.
p.   cm.
ISBN 0-87905-808-0
1. Cookies. 1. Title.
TX773.C69 1997
641.8' 654 – dc21
96-50416
CIP

WILD, WILD WEST

COWBOY COOKIES

TUDA LIBBY CREWS

Happy trails!
Tuda Libby Crews
NFR - 1998

GIBBS SMITH, PUBLISHER
SALT LAKE CITY

GIBBS·SMITH
PUBLISHER

ACKNOWLEDGEMENTS

I thank Grandmother Isabelle C de Baca, my life's touchstone. I learned about cooking from watching her devote endless hours to kitchen work, and she taught me about the importance of family. She taught me how to drive when I was ten years old. I honor and thank my mother, Esther Libby, a woman of grace, wisdom, and warmth, and my dearest friend. From our ranch kitchen, she was the hub of the wheel around which all activities flowed. I still feel her small warm hands in mine and recall a familiar skiff of flour across her fingers, a memory that continues to impart her strength and love.

I honor my family. I'm especially grateful for the love and support, and also the business counsel, from my dear husband, Jack. I appreciate his endurance of our home "test kitchen," and for eating all my broken cookies. I cherish my children. Thanks to Ted for his superb technical support, and to Libby and Peter for having faith in me. I hope they continue the rest of their lives to nurture that "little kid" within them. I look forward to decorating cowboy cookies with my grandchildren someday—please make it soon.

I've long been aware that my accomplishments are the result of enlisting help from my circle of incredible friends who share countless hours of their time and talent with me. I appreciate all the women from Civic League and from W-Heels who gathered to bake and decorate cowboy cookies for benefit events in the Cheyenne community. I'm grateful to cookbook author Beverly Cox for her time and expertise. And thank you, my author friend Teresa Jordan, for generously giving me direction and support in this cookbook effort. I appreciate the encouragement from my sisters, Mary Libby Campbell and Tacey Libby Levis, my champions and confidantes.

I'm crazy about Gibbs Smith and his publishing staff. I appreciate Jan Schou's high level of photography skills, the creative genius of book designer Scott Van Kampen, and the joyful play of dancing words from my friend and editor, Caroll McKanna Shreeve.

I fancy the cowboys whose dry repartee, love of cattle and horses, and close ties to the land connect me to them. Mighty grateful is what I am.

—TUDA LIBBY CREWS

CONTENTS

INTRODUCTION

THIS BOOK IS DEDICATED TO THE CHILDREN AND TO THE "LITTLE CHILD" IN EACH OF US.

ardner, the Old West comes to life in your kitchen as you mix, cut out, bake, and decorate *Wild, Wild West Cowboy Cookies*. Created for big and little "kids" who love the cowboy's way of life, this cookbook shows you how to create delightful western cookies. It includes a yummy lemon-flavored cookie dough recipe and a rich chocolate-flavored dough recipe, three delicious frosting recipes, and a wealth of information on how to decorate cowboy cookies. These decorating tips can be applied to cookies made for any occasion.

Cooking was a major part of daily activity where I was raised on a northeastern New Mexico ranch. Regular trips to the nearest grocery store, a seventy-five-mile drive one-way, replenished stockpiles of staples and fresh produce year-round. The isolated location of our ranch didn't deter the constant flow of visitors who often arrived at mealtime. My grandmother, Isabelle C de Baca, and my mother, Esther Libby, did the lion's share of the cooking and were experts in setting out delicious fare, even on very short notice.

Though the women capably worked alone, meal preparations were often done by people working together, with family members, visitors, hired men, and even little children pitching in. It was the norm for people to say, "What can I do to help?" I was brought up to realize that the secret to good cooking was love . . . love in your heart for your family and friends, love for the joy of nurturing them, and love for the work involved in preparing each meal. I vividly recall hearing my mother say, "Food is love made visible." Whether served on the large kitchen table or out in the pasture near the branding corral, mealtime, especially the noon meal called "dinner," was a celebration of food, fellowship, and ranch work.

Each day, dinner preparations filled our house with fragrant kitchen aromas. New Mexico pinto beans seasoned with salt pork were smothered with simmering red chili con carne, and thick slices of juicy beef roasts were served with mountains of freshly baked ranch rolls. There were crisp salads with ranch dressing, and rich brown gravy to ladle over potatoes. Freshly baked desserts, such as cookies, peach cobblers, pies, and cakes, especially chocolate ones, followed the meal. My heart warms and my mouth waters at the memory of sharing delicious food with so many fine folks. Cowboy camaraderie stimulated laughter and endless embellished stories around the table.

At the ranch there was always a pot of coffee on the stove and a sweet to offer company. Cookies were plentiful. Among my grandma's cookie specialties were tasty mincemeat, oatmeal, and a delicate jelly-filled sugar cookie. I especially remember my grandmother's *Biscochitos*, a recipe flavored with anise seed that calls for two cups of lard and yields a fleur-de-lis-shaped shortbreadlike cookie. Biscochitos are a New Mexico

Christmas tradition following midnight mass and are always served with hot coffee to friends gathered in the kitchen. My mother made a delicious cakelike applesauce-raisin cookie that stands out in my mind. She made cutout cookies for us at Christmas, Halloween, Thanksgiving, and Easter, and from early childhood, we children always helped decorate them.

So I come from a family of cooks, and I come from a cookie-loving family. My grandmother and mother were cookie mothers, and I'm carrying on the tradition. I began when my children, Libby and Ted, were very young. In our kitchen, we mixed and cut out and baked and decorated while we created warm childhood memories. Often, several of their friends came over to help bake holiday cookies. The children had great fun eating dough, cutting out shapes, and creating splashy frosting combinations. Throughout their grade-school years, I volunteered to serve as a room-mother, decorating bright orange jack-o'-lanterns at Halloween and green Christmas trees for their class parties.

My cowboy cookies evolved long after my children grew up and left home. A longtime cookie-cutter collector, I happened to buy some new cutter shapes when I was visiting my son in Arizona. A chili pepper cutter caught my eye, and I thought it would be fun to serve red-and-green chili-shaped cookies for dessert with one of my Mexican dinners! I ran across an exceptionally well-shaped cowboy boot and bought it because it appeared so real. I also bought a longhorn steer head and a cactus, envisioning how charming they could look frosted to make them appear lifelike. When I returned home, I set about doing just that.

I mixed vivid frosting colors, practiced applying frosting through a piping tube, and with imagination created some unique western cookies that looked dramatically "real." When our son, Ted, graduated from Arizona State University, I baked and decorated dozens of cowboy cookies for his party. It was great fun to serve them and delight family and friends with my creative confections. I was touched when many of the guests carefully carried cookies home to preserve and hang on their Christmas trees.

In the fall of 1993, a group of Cheyenne friends gathered to bake and decorate forty dozen cowboy cookies for a fund-raiser benefitting our community's Cheyenne Frontier Days Old West Museum. The event showcased Teresa Jordan, a gifted young author from Iron Mountain, Wyoming, who gave a reading from her successful book *Riding the White Horse Home.* Dozens of carefully decorated white horses herded by outfitted riders filled large silver platters. They were a huge hit with little and big "kids." Guests also enjoyed the colorful assortment of hats, guitars, coyotes, cowboy boots, and cactus shapes!

Later that year about a dozen members of the Cheyenne Women's Civic League gathered to bake, decorate, and donate another forty dozen cowboy cookies for Christmas House, a well-established fund-raiser that annually benefits community projects. The cowboy cookies were a sellout. Again, through volunteerism and caring people, the cookie-making project reflected that warm and true spirit so typical of the West.

One day while waiting in the dentist's office, I was browsing through a *Better Homes & Gardens* magazine and read about a forthcoming cookie-decorating contest. Riding high on the recent winds of local notoriety, I submitted my cowboy cookie decorating entry later that day. I was confident of winning the $2,500 cash prize, so confident that I had a contractor drive out to our home and give me an estimate on replacing my kitchen cabinets. I patiently waited until spring for the contest results. Finally, I received a letter from the magazine informing me that my entry did not win. However, they asked if I would be interested in allowing them to print a story on the cookies in some future issue for the sum of one hundred dollars. Discouraged, I replied no to the offer. Little did I realize at the time how true it is that when one door closes, another door opens.

Months later, Janet Figg, editor of the *Better Homes & Gardens* Special Interest Publications contacted me and asked to use my cowboy cookies as a full-color feature article in the *Christmas Cookies 1995* issue. I agreed to a one-time use. I experienced a memorable trip to Des Moines, Iowa, through a raging spring blizzard to work in Meredith Corporation's professional kitchen. Their terrific staff and talented photographer created a marvelous color layout for my cowboy cookies. Fan mail response to the cookie feature was very favorable, so I decided to pursue my concept as a cookbook.

I submitted a *Wild, Wild West* *Cowboy Cookies* cookbook proposal to Gibbs Smith, Publisher, and included samples of my colorfully decorated cowboy cookies. They enthusiastically accepted my idea, and we began negotiating a contract. I'm continually amazed at what exciting things have happened since I didn't win that cookie-decorating contest.

Wild, Wild West Cowboy Cookies came about because of my deep love for my family's ranch and the cowboy way of life and also because of that little cowgirl that continues to live happily in my heart. I hope you corral a herd of kids for a fun and happy experience making cutout, decorated cowboy cookies for parties, holidays, or for your child's sack lunch for school.

I hope this cookie cookbook becomes one of your favorites—and now, enjoy! May your ovens bake golden-edged cookies whose fragrance lingers, warming hearts young and old, and may your kitchen be a loving place for creating lasting childhood memories for children you love. I'm proud and happy to share with you the secrets of my charming cowboy cookies and my collector's edition of cowboy cookie cutters. By the way, I'm still planning for new kitchen cabinets somewhere along the trail. ❦

DOUGHS

COWBOY COOKIE DOUGH

EVERY BUCKAROO'S DREAM COME TRUE

 elebrating the West and the cowboy way of life, these elaborately decorated western cowboy cookies keep well, or at least until little buckaroos get the munchies! At last, a sugar cookie that is delicious and does not break easily. Perfect for decorating!

Use a heavy-duty mixer or food processor for this large batch. The recipe is easily cut in half for a small electric mixer or for hand mixing.

PHOTOGRAPH BY JOE COCA

- 8 cups flour
- ½ teaspoon cream of tartar
- ½ teaspoon salt
- 2 teaspoons baking soda
- 2 ½ cups sugar
- ¾ cup butter
- ¾ cup butter-flavored vegetable shortening
- Rind of 1 large lemon, grated
- 4 medium eggs
- 2 teaspoons vanilla (Mexican vanilla preferred)
- 1 cup evaporated milk (or whipping cream)
- Extra flour for rolling out dough

Sift flour and measure into a large bowl. With a wire whisk, thoroughly mix together the flour, cream of tartar, salt, and soda. Set aside.

Cream together the sugar, butter, and vegetable shortening until light and fluffy. Add the lemon rind and eggs, and continue mixing. Stir vanilla into the evaporated milk and add to mixture, beating until smooth.

Add sifted dry ingredients one cup at a time, mixing well after each addition to form a stiff ball of dough.

Place dough on a floured surface. Divide into three parts. Place each mound on a piece of plastic wrap. Using your hands, shape each mound into a smooth, flat, 1-inch-thick circle. Wrap each flat circle with plastic and allow to chill in refrigerator for thirty minutes.

Set oven temperature to 350° F.

See Part II: Tips & Techniques for rolling out dough, cutting out shapes, baking, and frosting the finished cookies.

Yield: approximately 7 dozen cookies.

CHOCOLATE
BUFFALO DOUGH

Use a heavy-duty mixer or food processor for this large batch. The recipe is easily cut in half for a small electric mixer or for mixing by hand.

- 8 ½ cups flour
- ½ teaspoon cream of tartar
- ½ teaspoon salt
- 2 teaspoons baking soda
- (10) 1-ounce squares of unsweetened chocolate
- 3 cups sugar
- ½ cup butter
- ½ cup butter-flavored vegetable shortening
- 3 eggs
- 3 teaspoons vanilla
- 1 cup evaporated milk (or whipping cream)
- Extra flour for rolling out dough

Sift the flour and measure into a large bowl. Add the cream of tartar, salt, and soda; mix dry ingredients together with a wire whisk and set aside.

Melt the chocolate squares over medium-low heat in a saucepan, or on medium temperature in a microwave oven.

Cream together the sugar, butter, and vegetable shortening until light and fluffy. Add the melted chocolate. Add the eggs one at a time, mixing well after each addition. Stir vanilla into evaporated milk and add to the mixture, beating until smooth.

Add sifted dry ingredients one cup at a time, and mix well after each addition to form a stiff dough.

Place dough on a floured surface. Divide into three parts. Place each mound on a piece of plastic wrap and shape into a smooth, flat, 1-inch-thick circle with your hands. Wrap each circle with plastic wrap and allow to chill in refrigerator for thirty minutes. Do not refrigerate this dough for longer than thirty minutes before rolling out. Its rich and heavy texture becomes hard to work with if too cold.

Set oven temperature to 350° F.

See Part II: Tips & Techniques for rolling out dough, cutting out shapes, baking, and frosting the finished cookies.

Yield: approximately 7 dozen cookies.

Chocolate Buffalo Dough may be stored frozen for up to six weeks. After freezing, allow dough to thaw to room temperature before rolling it out. ❧

ADOBE FROSTING

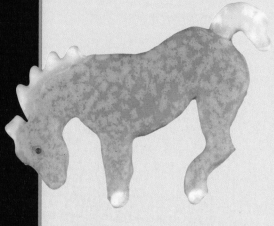

The light tan color of this frosting is perfect for creating adobe mission churches, palomino ponies, guitars, roping steers, cowboy hats and boots, and for accents on other special critters!

Place a saucepan over low heat and melt butter. Stir brown sugar into melted butter. Bring to a low boil and then stir in evaporated milk. Stirring often, bring mixture to a soft boil and remove from heat. Place in the bowl of an electric mixer; add confectioners' sugar and beat until light and fluffy. Add very hot water, one tablespoon at a time, to thin the mixture to a soft spreading consistency.

Read Decorating Tips starting on page 29 before you begin to decorate your cowboy cookies.

- 1 cup butter
- 2 cups dark brown sugar, packed
- ½ cup evaporated skimmed milk
- 4 cups confectioners' sugar, sifted
- Water, very hot, as needed

Yield: approximately 3 cups frosting.

PHOTOGRAPH BY
JOE COCA

FUDGY CHOCOLATE FROSTING

This delicious chocolate frosting is ideal for coloring buffalo, bucking ponies, cowboy hats and boots, and for decorative accents on other special critters!

- ■ ½ cup butter
- ■ (6) 1-ounce squares of unsweetened chocolate
- ■ 7 cups confectioners' sugar, sifted
- ■ ¾ cup coffee or water, hot
- ■ 2 teaspoons vanilla (Mexican preferred)
- ■ 3 bottles chocolate sprinkles (for decorating buffalo manes and tails)

Place a saucepan over low heat and melt butter and chocolate, mixing together until thoroughly blended. Place mixture in the bowl of an electric mixer and add remaining ingredients; beat on high until well blended. Add additional hot coffee or hot water, one tablespoon at a time, until a soft spreading consistency is reached.

Read Decorating Tips starting on page 29 before you begin to decorate your buffalo cookies.

Yield: approximately 4 cups frosting.

SUGAR-BABY FROSTING

- (1) 32-ounce package confectioners' sugar, sifted
- ⅓ cup evaporated skimmed milk
- ⅓ cup white corn syrup
- 1 teaspoon vanilla (Mexican preferred)
- ⅓ cup water, boiling

Use a heavy-duty mixer for a double recipe of frosting.

Sift confectioners' sugar and set aside.

Combine evaporated milk, corn syrup, and vanilla in a small saucepan over heat; then place this hot liquid in a mixing bowl. Immediately add boiling water and blend with electric mixer on low speed.

Add sifted confectioners' sugar and continue blending on low speed until a smooth, soft consistency is achieved. Tightly cover the bowl with plastic wrap to prevent crystals from forming over the top of the frosting.

Yield: approximately 3 cups frosting.

The ideal consistency of Sugar-Baby Frosting is similar to a petits-fours glaze. To check the consistency, run a spoon down the center of the frosting from one end of the bowl to the other. If the consistency is right, the frosting should hold the split for 5 or 6 seconds. Soft frosting makes spreading easier. Hold the frosting at a lukewarm temperature over a bowl of hot tap water. To soften, add boiling water one tablespoon at a time. To thicken, add sifted confectioners' sugar in small amounts until desired consistency is achieved. Read Decorating Tips starting on page 29 before you begin to color the frosting and to decorate your cowboy cookies. ❧

Cowboy Cookies

Cowboy Cookies are
A sight for sore eyes,
A treat for disciminatin'
Cowgirls and cowguys.

For lots of fun and laughter
Goes into the bakin'
And only the most clever
Do the decoratin'.

We gaily paint howlin' coyotes
In brightly colored hues
An set 'em on platters with Buffaloes,
Mission Churches, and Buckaroos

And Steers, Hats 'n' Horses
Are sugar coated with delight;
Sometimes the frosting work
Lasts long into the night.

Each cookie is indeed a gift
Though it sure takes lots of practice
To get the saddle stitching on the boots
And flowers on all the cactus

But Cheyenne gals don't mind
Creatin' Cowboy Cookies
'Cause we know how much they're appreciated
By those Western-lovin' rookies!

TUDA CREWS © 1993

19

Part Two: Tips & Techniques

fter the dough has chilled, cut a sheet of plastic wrap approximately 18 inches long and lay it flat on the work surface. Lightly sprinkle the plastic wrap with flour. Place a completely unwrapped circle of chilled cookie dough onto the floured plastic wrap. Lightly flour the top of the dough. Cut another 18-inch-long piece of plastic wrap and smooth it over the top of the floured circle of dough. Using the plastic wrap prevents the dough from sticking to the rolling pin and gives the dough surface a smooth texture.

Starting from the center and working to the outside, roll out the dough in short gentle strokes moving completely around the circle, rotating the rolling pin clockwise as you work to prevent the dough from splitting around the edges. You may have to lift and smooth the plas-tic wrap to eliminate wrinkles that can mar the smooth dough surface. Roll out the dough to approximately 1/4-inch thickness. Remove the top layer of plastic and grasp the bottom piece of plastic; flip the rolled-out circle of dough so that the bottom plastic is now on top. Remove the remaining plastic and use the rolling pin to give the dough a final smoothing touch.

After all the shapes are cut out, gather the scraps of dough into a ball and knead 6 or 8 times, or until the ball appears smooth. Wrap the dough in plastic wrap and allow it to rest for at least thirty minutes before you roll it out again. After the second rolling, the dough tends to become tough. It is a good idea to use this dough for practicing frosting techniques for the cookies, or roll out and cut the dough into squares for cookie samples.

CUTTING-OUT TIPS

⚜ Before cutting out the cookies, prepare lightly greased cookie sheets, or, to save cleanup time, cover the bottom of each sheet with parchment paper.

⚜ Use the entire surface of the rolled-out dough to get the maximum number of shapes from your circle. Cut out the cookie shapes by placing the cutter as close as possible to the last shape removed from the dough. Place the cutter down firmly—flat on the dough—and give it a wiggle back and forth. The movement makes the dough come away from the inside edges of the cutter and it is easier to remove the cutter without breaking the cookie shape. After you cut out the primary shapes, select a small cutter to use for the remaining dough.

⚜ If the cutter has narrow places in the design (for example, the legs of the buffalo), try this tip: as you lift the cutter away, gently push the dough down inside the cookie shape with the point of a small sharp knife or skewer to keep the legs from breaking off. If a cookie loses one of its parts, mend it by dampening the broken edges of the dough with a little water and carefully patting it back together again. The moisture helps the broken piece to seal into place during baking.

⚜ For professional results, carefully lift the cutout cookies with a spatula and arrange them on lightly greased cookie sheets at least one inch apart so cookies do not expand and grow together as they bake. If a shape becomes distorted when you move it onto the cookie sheet, use a spatula or a knife edge to straighten the cookie. To assure well-shaped cookies and a professional finished product, carefully remove dough crumbs from the edges of the cookie shapes before baking. ⚜

For best results, bake the cookies one sheet at a time for 8 to 9 minutes. Cookies are done when you touch the cookie lightly and it springs back. The edges may appear slightly golden. Do not over-bake; cookies tend to break too easily when overcooked.

When the cookies come out of the oven, remove them from the sheet with a spatula and place them on waxed or parchment paper immediately so they don't continue to bake. Allow time for the cookies to cool before frosting them.

BASIC DECORATING SUPPLIES

🦌 Organize plenty of work space in a well-lighted area near a kitchen sink.

🦌 Spread frostings with a half dozen ordinary dinnerware knives or butter knives.

🦌 Keep plenty of clean damp cloths on hand to use for wiping off the edges of the knife blades and the ends of the piping tubes.

🦌 Purchase professional, disposable, plastic decorating tubes, holders, and twist-on rings to hold the tips in place. Have a selection of piping colors ready. For best results, apply the contrasting colors of piping with at least six metal tips in sizes 3 and 4. Having frosting tubes prepared in a variety of colors and tip sizes saves time in applying frosting detail as you switch from one cookie design to another

🦌 Have on hand plenty of waxed paper, plastic wrap, spatulas, and cookie sheets.

🦌 Purchase Candy-n-Cake™ powdered food colors to mix brilliant frosting colors.

PHOTOGRAPH BY JOE COCA

BASIC FROSTING TECHNIQUES

DIPPING BACKGROUND FROSTINGS

Use Fudgy Chocolate Frosting, Adobe Frosting, or mix background colors with Sugar-Baby Frosting in tints of red, green, yellow, blue, hot pink, violet, turquoise, and other favorites.

To apply professional-looking background colors, select a container with an opening that provides a surface broad enough to dip the entire cookie, then pour in the desired colored frosting. Using your left hand, place your thumb and middle finger on the outside edges of the cookie, and, holding it gently, dip the top surface into the desired background color of frosting. When you raise the cookie out of the frosting, angle it downward and gently smooth the excess frosting from the surface of the cookie with the blade of a dinnerware knife, allowing the excess frosting to fall back into the frosting dish.

With a clean knife edge, run the blade around the entire outside of the cookie to remove any excess frosting. Place the

cookie on waxed paper to set-up. If a large run of frosting builds up as the frosting begins to set, carefully raise the cookie by slipping a spatula underneath to avoid marring the frosting with your fingers, then lay the cookie in your outstretched fingers and palm. Hold the cookie in your hand and gently remove the excess frosting with a clean knife edge. The goal is to have a smooth frosted surface and edge to each cookie. A little practice makes it easy.

✦ Place the frosted cookie on waxed paper. Check to see if a run of frosting has gone over the edge of the cookie. If this has occurred, carefully lift the cookie again with your spatula and fingers and remove the excess with a clean knife edge. Allow each frosted cookie to set up completely before moving it.

✦ As you work, maintain the lukewarm temperature of the frosting.

✦ To obtain professional results with these frostings, follow these suggestions carefully: If the bowl of frosting is left uncovered,

a thin wall of crystals may form over the surface, or small lumps may appear as you are decorating a cookie. If this occurs, stop decorating. Dissolve the crystals by gently adding $\frac{1}{2}$ inch of very hot water to cover the entire surface of the frosting in its container. Allow the hot water to remain for ten seconds and then pour off the entire amount. After the excess is poured off, the thin film of water at the top is often sufficient liquid to stir the frosting back to the desirable spreading consistency. Use this trick to soften the various colored frostings as you work to keep them smooth and prevent sugar crystals from forming. Keep the frosting covered between dipping steps. As you work, stir the frosting to keep it smooth and to prevent sugar crystals from forming.

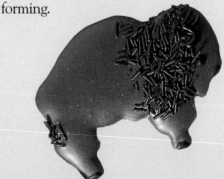

PIPING DESIGN-DETAIL FROSTINGS

Mix vivid contrasting shades of orange, black, or purple frosting for applying piping detail over background colors. Deeper tones of piping create the most dramatic effect. Let your imagination run mustang-free in wild color combinations.

It is important to remember that the frosting used to fill the piping tube must be thicker than the frosting mixed for the background colors. Add sifted confectioners' sugar by the tablespoon until folds of the frosting remain observable when you stir through the mixture. A fairly stiff consistency is desirable.

To fill the piping tube, turn the top of the piping tube inside-out to halfway down the tube. Adjust the piping tube overhang over a tall glass with the metal point and ring hanging inside. Spread the opening and use a spoon to place the frosting in the plastic tube.

Remove the tube from the glass and use your hands to squeeze the frosting to the very bottom until the frosting begins to come out of the decorating tip. Gather the ends of the plastic tube and twist tightly to hold the frosting in place and secure the ends with a baggy twist.

When applying the piping, squeeze the frosting out from the end of the bag, twisting to take up the slack as you work.

🦌 If the frosting is too thick to squeeze from the piping tube, run a little hot water over the outside of the plastic bag to soften it occasionally. If the frosting in the filled tube is too runny, chill it in the refrigerator for a few minutes. Ideal consistency is achieved when piping flows from the tube and adheres itself to the colored background surface of the cookie.

🦌 To practice applying designs using the piping tube, wrap a piece of clear plastic wrap over a cookie. Pipe the design onto the clear plastic and see if you like it. If not, simply toss the practice plastic wrap away and try again. You can become very proficient with a little practice.

WILD, WILD WEST FROSTING TIPS

ADOBE FROSTING TIPS

Adobe Frosting makes a great background for the Mission Church cookie! Try piping white Sugar-Baby Frosting in the windows and Fudgy Chocolate Frosting for accents on the doors and the cross!

Adobe Frosting makes a great background for the roping steer, the palomino pony, and the Great White Buffalo!

Buff-colored Adobe Frosting ponies can be spotted or solid!

FUDGY CHOCOLATE FROSTING TIPS

⤴ For Chocolate Buffalo Cookies, hold the freshly dipped cookie over a plate and generously shake chocolate sprinkles over the buffalo's head and neck, his hump, and shoulders. The sprinkles quickly stick to the soft frosting.

⤴ To designate his tail, pick up a few chocolate sprinkles with your fingers and press them into the area at the back of his rump (remember, buffalo have short tails!). Unlike applying decorative piping when the background frosting is completely dry as previously described, it is important to apply the sprinkles while the background frosting is still soft, or they will not stick unless pressed into the frosting, which cracks it and mars the sur-

face. Fudgy Chocolate Frosting and sprinkles make woolly brown buffaloes look real!

⤴ The final touch is to add little black hooves, a black nose, an eye, and a horn. Buffalo horns grow back toward the neck and then curl upwards quickly. Dozens of buffalo cookies are stunning served on a large plank or a platter as a whole "herd."

⤴ See Sugar-Baby Frosting Tips for other ideas about creating wild, wild buffaloes!

SUGAR-BABY FROSTING TIPS

✦ Set aside ½ cup of white Sugar-Baby Frosting for one background tint, then divide the remainder of the frosting into covered containers for mixing. Allow at least ¾ cup of frosting to dip the cookies in for background colors and ½ cup of colored frosting to fill each piping tube.

✦ Purchase Candy-n-Cake™ powdered food colors to mix brilliant frosting colors. For the most dramatic effect, add powdered color to the white Sugar-Baby Frosting until you reach a vivid hue. A rule of thumb applies to the coloring process: add ½ teaspoon of powdered color to ½ cup of frosting and stir well until the powder is dissolved. Continue to add powdered color in ½-teaspoon increments, stirring well after each addition, until the desired shade is achieved. For example, add 1½ teaspoons of yellow powder to ½ cup of frosting to achieve a brilliant yellow hue for hot-colored guitars, boots, or colorful Fiesta Buffalo Gals.

✦ You can add a special touch to your presentation of buffalo cookies by including a single Great White Buffalo, the

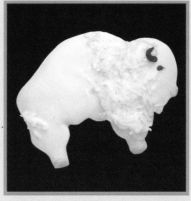

PHOTOGRAPH BY JOE COCA

Native American symbol of the White Calf Buffalo Woman who brought the sacred pipe to her people. Cut out the white buffalo from Cowboy Cookie Dough and dip it in white Sugar-Baby Frosting. Immediately decorate it with shredded coconut over the hump, shoulders, and a little over the top of its head. Make the horns, nose, and hooves of light Adobe Frosting to complete the albino appearance. Shredded coconut brings the furry Great White Buffalo to life!

🦌 Wild 'n' crazy people sometimes make Fiesta Buffalo Gals red, purple, and hot pink! Vary the look of your buffaloes by dipping them in bright-colored Sugar-Baby Frosting for a fun fiesta-colors effect. Enhance the impact of your wild, wild buffalo shapes with hot-pink noses, horns, hooves, and matching

colored-sugar sprinkles for the hump, mane, and tail. Remember, practice makes perfect and you can create your "signature" cookie by experimenting imaginatively.

🦌 Decorative Native American contrasting lines and "beadwork" of cookie-decorating candies make sophisticated designs with great audience appeal.

🦌 For a stunning presentation, the plate or tray background of the buffalo herd may be turquoise, hot yellow, hot pink, or other bright fiesta colors.

A SADDLEBAG OF ASSORTED DECORATING TIPS

🐎 If pressed for time, any brand of low-fat canned frosting can be substituted for the recipes in this book. Low-fat frosting is preferred, because the higher-fat-content frostings tend to mottle the bright colors.

🐎 Don't forget blue jeans and a red shirt on the bucking bronc rider!

🐎 Don't forget to saddle-stitch the cowboy boots!

🐎 Chilies come in yellow, red, or green, and hot fiesta colors look great, too!

🐎 Get wild with a bright selection of gila monster lizards!

🐎 With howlin' coyotes, anything goes; just make 'em so bright you almost have to close your eyes to take a bite!

🐎 Cactus are a light shade of green! Put lots of bright colors in the flowers!

🐎 Guitars can be frosted in hot colors, adobe, or chocolate! Pay special attention to contrasting colors in piped frosting for the string details.

🐎 Give your imagination free rein and see what wonderful cookies you can create and what delightful displays you can have fun with against bright cowboy bandannas, rough wood, or tooled leather surfaces. Use the pictures in this book for display ideas. 🌱

For large quantities, particularly when the cookies are to be stored or shipped, it is a good idea to bake them in advance and decorate them at a later date.

If cookies, frosted or unfrosted, become too brittle to be appetizing, experiment in your climate with storing them in a plastic container with one or two slices of fresh white bread. Place the bread slices on the bottom of the container and one layer of cookies on a cookie rack over them. Close the lid firmly. In three or four hours, the cookies will be soft and delicious without any change in their flavor.

Undecorated, the cookies freeze very well for up to two months. Place them in an airtight container with sheets of wax paper and cut-to-fit pieces of poster board between each layer to prevent breakage.

Packed in the same manner, frosted cookies can be stored up to two weeks in an airtight container in a cool place out of direct light. Light and heat may mottle some frosting colors. It is best not to freeze cookies after they are frosted as the frosting changes color from the moisture. Extremes of heat or cold distort the professional appearance of the product. ❧

PHOTOGRAPHS BY JOE COCA

SHIPPING COWBOY COOKIES

If you pack cowboy cookies properly, they ship very well. Select an appropriate size box and line the bottom with bubble-wrap to absorb shock. Cut a large piece of plastic wrap to lay over the bubble-wrap in the bottom and around the sides of the box. Layer plastic wrap, cut-to-fit poster board, more bubble-wrap, then cookies, allowing extra space at the top for a thick layer of bubble-wrap. After all the cookies are packed, bring the plastic ends together to enclose all the layers of cookies inside to keep them fresh while being shipped. Cookies may be wrapped individually in plastic wrap and tied with a ribbon or attractively arranged on the flat surface of the cushion of bubble-wrap. This provides padding and evenly distributes the weight of the cookies, preventing breakage. Place a lining of bubble-wrap over the top layer before you put the lid on. Tie or tape the box closed and add an additional wrapping of bubble-wrap around the entire package. Place the package inside a corrugated cardboard box with additional packing to make it fit snugly inside. The cookies can be shipped overnight express or sent through the mail.

PHOTOGRAPH BY JOE COCA

Part Three: Tools, Transfers & Sources

uda Crews teaches the art of decorating Wild, Wild West Cowboy Cookies in workshops and demonstrations across the country. Sharing a fun and challenging hobby with her husband, Jack, they hitch up their Y Mill Iron chuckwagon and compete in chuckwagon cook-offs in New Mexico and Texas. In Wyoming and beyond, the cooking team has earned an award-winning reputation for stirring up delicious cowboy fare at special events.

PHOTOGRAPH BY JOE COCA

USING TRANSFERS

Trace onto baking parchment, cut out templates, and transfer onto rolled-out dough. Pipe frosting details as indicated. ❧

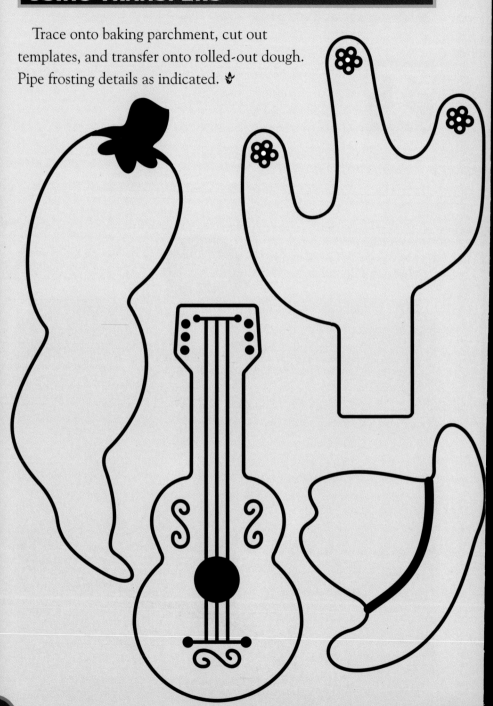

The following sources carry powdered food coloring, disposable frosting tubes, piping tips, plastic inserts and rings, chocolate sprinkles, and brilliantly colored sugar crystals for decorating Wild, Wild West Cowboy Cookies:

KING ARTHUR™ FLOUR BAKER'S CATALOGUE

P.O. Box 876
Norwich, VT 05055

(800) 827-6836
Fax: (800) 343-3002

HOBBY LOBBY™ STORES, INC.

SWEET CELEBRATIONS, INC.™ CATALOG

P.O. Box 39426
Edina, MN 55439

(800) 328-6722
Twin City Metro Area &
outside USA (612) 943-1508

DENISE'S

Cake & Candy Supplies
4963 South Peoria
Tulsa, OK 74105

(918) 747-2266

WHOLESALE SUPPLIER

APOLLO MOLD COMPANY, INC.

5546 South Colombia Avenue
Tulsa, OK 74105

(918) 258-9595
Fax: (918) 258-9597

COURTESY LIST OF BOOKS TO READ

The author highly recommends the following books:

DEBBI FIELDS GREAT AMERICAN DESSERTS

Simon & Schuster
1230 Avenue of the Americas
New York, NY 10020
Copyright © 1996 by Debbi Fields
and Reid / Lane Productions

To order, call (800) 331-1000

SPIRIT OF THE WEST, COOKING FROM RANCH HOUSE AND RANGE

by Beverly Cox and Martin Jacobs
Artisan Publishing, a division of
Workman Publishing, Inc.
708 Broadway
New York, NY 10003-9555

To order, call Joe Pages Bookstore
& Coffee House (307) 778-7134

CHUCKWAGON RECIPES & OTHERS

by Sue Cunningham and Jean Cates
P.O. Box 22
Hartley, TX 79044

To order, call (806) 365-4596

RIDING THE WHITE HORSE HOME

by Teresa Jordan
Pantheon Books
201 E. 50th St.
New York, NY 10022

To order, call (800) 733-3000

COWBOY POETRY, A GATHERING

edited and with an introduction
by Hal Cannon
Gibbs Smith, Publisher
P.O. Box 667
Layton, UT 84041

To order, call (800) 748-5439
Fax: (800) 213-3023 ❧

WILD WEST CUTTERS ORDER FORM

ORDER BY:
Be sure to fill form in completely

Name _____

Address _____

City _____ State _____ Zip _____

Home phone _____

Evening phone _____

SHIPPING ADDRESS: (if different)

Name _____

C/O _____

Address _____

City _____ State _____ Zip _____

METHOD OF PAYMENT

☐ Check or money order enclosed
☐ Visa: Card Number ⌶⌶⌶⌶⌶⌶⌶⌶ Expiration date ____
Signature as shown on Credit Card ____

ORDER INFORMATION

ITEM NUMBER	DESCRIPTIONS	HOW MANY?	PRICE EACH (Dollars / Cents)	TOTAL PRICE (Dollars / Cents)
01 CE	Cowboy on bronco		$19.95	
02 CE	Buffalo		$15.95	
03 CE	Boot		$14.95	
04	Standing cowboy		$3.00	
05	Saquaro cactus		$3.00	
06	Cowboy hat		$3.00	
07	Longhorn steer		$3.00	
08	Chili pepper		$3.00	
09	Howling coyote		$3.00	
10	Bucking pony		$6.00	
11	Chuckwagon		$6.00	
12	Mission church		$6.00	
13	Gecko lizard		$6.00	

TOTAL FOR MERCHANDISE

Wyoming Shipments add 5%.
Add applicable sales tax.

ADD FOR SHIPPING & HANDLING
(see chart at left)
☐ SURFACE
☐ BLUE LABEL
☐ RED LABEL

TOTAL AMOUNT ENCLOSED

SHIPPING AND HANDLING CHARGES:

UPS is the standard methods for continental USA shipments.
US PARCEL POST is the standard method for Hawaii, Alaska. (USA by request)

ORDER TOTAL	SURFACE 9-12 Working Days	UPS BLUE LABEL 3 Days	UPS RED LABEL 2 Working Days
$00.00 to $30.00	$3.75	$5.75	$15.75
$30 01 to $60.00	$5.95	$7.95	$17.95
$60 01 to $100.00	$7.75	$9.75	$19.75
$100 01 to $200.00	$9.25	$11.25	$21.25
OVER $200.00			

Mailing address for order form:

WILD WEST CUTTERS

P.O. Box 1804

Cheyenne WY 82003-1804

Place orders to this toll free
fax number: 1-888-277-0294

Web page address:
www.wildwestcookies.com

For further information,

write to this e-mail address:
info@wildwestcookies.com

Allow three weeks for delivery

WILD WEST CUTTERS

P.O. Box 1804 ✾ Cheyenne WY 82003-1804

Place orders to this toll free
fax number: 1-888-277-0294

Web page address:
www.wildwestcookies.com

For further information,
write to this e-mail address:
info@wildwestcookies.com

COLLECTOR SERIES OF COWBOY CUTTERS

Owner of *The Cookie Cutter Shop,* Colorado designer and tin-smith, *Elenna Firme,* has lassoed and tied the Rocky Mountains' most authentic cowboy cutter shapes. In a western showdown of creativity and talent, Elenna's cowboy on bronco, buffalo, and cowboy boot are now offered to collectors, hand-crafted by renowned coppersmith, Michael Bonne. Each copper cutter is stamped with the Wild, Wild West Cowboy Cookie logo.

Michael Bonne handcrafts this trio of gleaming copper cowboy cookie cutters using antique hand- and foot-operated tools. His mastery of quality copper work speaks of time-honored traditions, and feature articles in popular lifestyle magazines tell his story. Michael's other copper designs are carried in fine kitchen stores and gift shops around the country and abroad, and in Michael's own catalog, *The Commentator.*

01CE	Cowboy on bronco (6-inch cutter)	$19.95
02CE	Buffalo (4-inch cutter)	$15.95
03CE	Boot (3-inch cutter)	$14.95

Other western and southwestern tin-outline 3-inch cutters offered for sale are:

04	Standing cowboy	$3.00
05	Saguaro cactus	$3.00
06	Cowboy hat	$3.00
07	Longhorn steer	$3.00
08	Chili pepper	$3.00
09	Howling coyote	$3.00

Tuda has also gathered a small herd of unique western tin-outline 4-inch designs stamped with the Wild, Wild West Cowboy Cookie cutter logo and available only through this source:

10	Bucking pony	$6.00
11	Chuckwagon	$6.00
12	Mission church	$6.00
13	Gecko lizard	$6.00

Allow three weeks for delivery